Song of the Mushroom

Song of the Mushroom

A collection of new poems by Lee Sangguk
Translated by Deborah Kim

버섯의 노래 이상국

K-Poet Series 041

ASIA

Contents

Father, at Evening	8
Just Because	10
One Leg	12
In the End	14
Pissers	16
The Mountain Village's Cross	18
Principles of the Sea	20
As if Washed	22
Misiryeong Letter	24
Misiryeong Letter	26
Rice Paddy Waters	28
The Sun and Moon Never Rest	30
To Be Beautiful	32

For Absolute Solitude	34
The Radish Seed Is Strong	36
That Country	38
Hello Goodbye, Earth	40
Sky Lake	42
Song of the Mushroom	44
Gardenias Are White	46
Poet's Note	49
Poet's Essay	53
Commentary	61
Praise for Lee Sangguk	71

SONG OF
THE MUSHROOM

POET

Father, at Evening

When I see smoke curl out from a house on a
 country road

I think of my father.

Leaning back after a meal

smoking with relish, cigarette clamped between
 his lips,

in the way ancient trees are disfigured

my father had many scars

but it was always too dark to see.

As he puffed out smoke like a chimney.

Just Because

I watched the donkey.

The donkey stared back at me.

Face heroically long and gallant

its black eyes were beautiful.

I felt sorry, just because.

One Leg

Without thinking I caught a grasshopper in a
 meadow, when suddenly it shed one leg and
 went on its way.
I didn't mean to do it, still it discarded its leg so
 languidly...

A person's leg can't grow back. Nonetheless if a
 demand is made from up above,
sometimes something akin to one leg must be
 given.

In the End

There's an old goblin who lives in my village,

he pretends to be friendly if you cross paths in the night but

the longer you stare the larger he grows and then

he'll take you down and take you away—it's his calling.

If one day you can't find me,

having spent my life watching the world pass

me by,

I hope you'll understand what became of me in the end.

Pissers

A neighborhood dog pisses on a telephone pole
and buries its scent.
Digging at the cement with its hind paw
it goes through the motions of a burial before
    going away.

Some zoologist once said
when birds and creatures sense danger
to reduce their weight
they piss as they make their escape.

Whenever I stand in front of a big crowd
I get the urge to piss.

The Mountain Village's Cross

A church opened in the mountain village and when its neon cross lit up, no tree, no beast could rest or sleep in its glaring light, and so the village's night delved into deeper valleys and drew out the thick darkness to blanket them. With the blood shed in the struggle between light and dark, the mountain village's cross blazed redder.

Principles of the Sea

The sack of sea salt was in the yard, crying.

Having crossed the world in its vast body

before reaching my home,

there were no ports unvisited

no peoples unmet.

Thinking of these things, the sea salt cried.

As if Washed

As if washed–
how desperate these words can be.

Like how a child delirious with fever all night
at daybreak
calls for their mother through cracked blistered
 lips
as if no fever had ever touched them,

like women on an embankment in spring
 longing for cotton,
like my sister washing radish stumps under
 running water,

Love fractured,
wounds nobody sees.

Ah, as if washed.

Misiryeong Letter

When I was young and tending the East Sea I
 shared out
countless pyeong of sea among the poor poets

I gave with such abandon that I ran out of sea
 to give

These days, it's the moon crossing into the
 beyond at dawn, or
Ulsanbawi Rock that I register in secret and
I can only look on, out of sight…

Misiryeong Letter

After an early dinner I went out into the yard-

geese flying, crossing Seorak.

Bearing life on a single wing,

not disturbing a single thing.

I want to go with them.

Rice Paddy Waters

Spring rain fell and filled the rice paddies.

The tadpoles grow into frogs and leave
the rice paddy waters empty
and the gray herons infatuated with me
spend their days flying aimlessly.

If the mountains rest a day
the skies descend to unfurl their clouds
and violets the color of my sister's daenggi
    ribbon
gather round and sit on the paddy
    embankments.

People have wept over rice paddy waters.
I too, came from there.

The Sun and Moon Never Rest

The work week has been five days long for ages but

even on Saturdays the world's chickens lay eggs and

even on Sunday mornings the rain falls.

Land is boundless and though brimming with nations,

looking down from the skies

each place looks like the other and each day like

the next,

even on weekends whales nurse their young,

regardless of the day, apples blush red and grow ripe.

To Be Beautiful

Grey herons, mallards, plovers, brown-eared
 bulbuls, great reed warblers, they all live in
 the bird sanctuary I frequent.
Without a doubt, the egret is the most beautiful
 of them of all.
Come what may, other birds shed their finery
 according to the seasons, they flock together
 in reeds or on sandbars, but the egret is ever
 bright white, ever solitary, and at the slightest
 sound flies high to the sky in horror.

To be beautiful is to be in danger.

For Absolute Solitude

A sunbae I know who likes to wander outdoors photographing flowers said to me, Since I'm a poet, let me tell you about a flower and a butterfly that only seeks out that flower. So, what I'm saying is this flower blooms only for this butterfly and this butterfly lives and dies longing for this flower. With those words he handed me several seeds, light as clouds and wind. However, for the butterfly that has never been to the tiny planter in my corner of this sprawling city, and for the flower that would await the butterfly that would never come, though spring came and went, I did not bury the seeds.

The Radish Seed Is Strong

It's said that if radish seeds aren't planted before Cheoseo,
all autumn may pass but they won't take root.
And so, to sprout or not rests with the seed's will.

It's humans, and only humans, who call this season Cheoseo,
who think they can name something
that emerges from the earth astride crickets' backs,
that rides in from the skies on clouds.

Slashing lines across the whole universe

to divide it into before and after
disturbs the natural order.
But the radish seed doesn't fear Cheoseo.
No matter how enormous the earth may be
it can't match something the size of a grain of
  sand.
The radish seed is strong.

That Country

Fields smell sweet when rice is threshed.
It's because the earth exerts itself.
There are still people planting seeds in spring
and singing in autumn.
My old-fashioned self loves that somewhere
the old ways still live on.
Just between us,
if you bury a single seed of rice it multiplies into
    hundreds of grains.
So it is with all that grows in earth.
It's basically a windfall.
There are many still oblivious to this.
That's why farming is a mystical
and secret thing.

I am from that country and
when rice is threshed I can smell it cooked
and the aroma gives me strength.

Hello Goodbye, Earth

In the dead of winter in a dark corner of the bus terminal, people smoked. Though driven out, the final children of gloom—

For the companies that put poisonous gas into air purifiers killing and sickening thousands, it's business as usual. Israel bombards Gaza with their beautiful missiles intent on destroying all Palestinian bloodlines, and as Japan releases radioactive water into the Pacific Ocean, you hold your tongue, oh Earth—

Driving people out, sick over wisps of cigarette smoke and singed sky, oh pitiful Earth.

Sky Lake

On the road,

even in the rain pooled in cows' hoofprints

clouds drift by, the stars of the night sky shine,

and nameless bugs live on.

Song of the Mushroom

I'm the homeless person of the woods,

child of the rain and wind.

I have neither house nor wife

in the shade of leaves I make a shelter of dewdrops

and take a brief rest

at night I count the stars

I am a drifter in that universe.

Gardenias Are White

The gardenia tree is dead.
I placed the pot in an empty room
and never looked in on them, it was
as though they'd dressed in burial shrouds
their verdant green leaves died steadily, all
    together.
What thoughts ran through their mind
at the sound of rain falling on the roof, or
at the sound that traveled through the wall of
    our family having meals together?
The gardenias are dead.
Without so much as a whimper they expired
without so much as a backward glance they
    departed.

I buried it.

I buried it deep within its body.

Gardenias are white.

Dead gardenias are whiter.

POET'S NOTE

For the most part, poets are people who call out by name the small, the insignificant, or what is forgotten. We build them homes or observe rituals of welcome and parting for what comes to us unexpectedly and what departs without a word.

I don't know why, but when I see ants crawling out onto the dry road, I want to give myself to the swarm. Or when I see earthworms disappearing into dust, I want to beg them, do not do that.

POET'S ESSAY

POET

Where Have All the Wild Rabbits Gone?

1.

I inherited the mountains and streams from my ancestors. Since I was born and raised in a farming household, I am imbued with the culture and emotions of farmers. Therefore, it is natural that within my poetry there is nature and the songs and language of people who live off the land.

On the occasions I return to my hometown, I can see the fields and terraced rice paddies that people once coveted and envied now lay abandoned or have been reclaimed by the trees. What a waste. That land once nourished our people; seeing it abandoned and treated with such disregard is disrespectful. In times of drought, we spent all night filling up the rice paddies with water and herding away birds. These days, I can work a single day and earn enough to buy months' worth of rice. But that doesn't mean I'm happier.

For instance, my writing is imbued with mountains and streams, the lives of the people of that land, and their work songs. At times I call this traditional culture and I also think of it as folk sentiment. And so, the background of my poetry is the mountains and rivers, farmland and labor. Just as I spent my childhood waiting out the night by candlelight for the cow to give birth to the calf, no matter what I write, I know that supporting my work, that background is there and it is an enormous asset. As I mentioned, regardless of what I write, I can simply take and use the mountains and streams. They are inexhaustible raw materials. They cannot run out and they cost nothing. This can be said of my writings and of my life itself.

> I use and discard
> each beautiful day of my life
> like a roll of toilet paper.
> The universe refills it and sends it back to me, so
> each year spring feels like a new spring,
> each love feels like a new love,
> even death is yet like the first flood,
> so all I can do is use my life industriously.
> —Lee Sangguk, "Refill" From *Some Farmer's* Planet
> (Changbi, 2005)

2.

The polar bear chose to wear nature's white. It must have taken a long time, ambling along streams and mountains, trying on this and that color. It's beautiful and marvelous to see the polar bear trudging along snowy fields and over ice in his white garments. But as glaciers melt, it's said that catching prey is growing more difficult. It would be a sad sight, the polar bear with its cubs in tow, staring off into the distance after losing its prey. Without its months-long hibernation, survival might be even more difficult for the bear. However, this isn't the time to worry about bears. When the natural order is lost, humans will be next.

Scott Nearing said that nature is tireless, dogged, and merciless. Nearing's philosophy is the same as Zhang Zhou's thoughts on the impartiality of heaven and earth. Zhang Zhou asserted that the workings of heaven, of life and natural order, are Tao. To live following this order is the best way to lead life. And so, when Tao is filled it will return. To be full means to be empty.

Duanmu Ci once encountered a farmer who was watering his field manually. Duanmu Ci asked the farmer why he was using such a grueling method when a bucket and pulley tool could make his work easier. The farmer replied that if he used such a tool or machinery, then one day machines would be needed for work, and if machines are necessary, then the desire for machines would inevitably follow. This story is recounted in Zhuangzi. Though symbolic of productivity and idleness, another meaning is that the desire for machines because of greed disturbs the natural heart of humanity. People have long since gone beyond the desire for machines. Going one step further, with how the world's warehouses are full of weapons of war, it could be said that humanity is full of the desire for weapons

This so-called civilization is just another form of barbarism; it has weighed down and polluted this rock we live on called Earth. However, from a cosmic perspective, Earth turns with no ulterior motives and may be doing nothing more than playing house with this tiny species called human.

3.

Last winter, there were heavy snows where I live in Yeongdong, Gangwon. But I couldn't find a single wild rabbit's footprints anywhere. Where have all the wild rabbits gone?

COMMENTARY

Seeds Light as Clouds and Wind

Ahn Sang-Hak (Poet)

There is said to be a flower that blooms in waiting for one butterfly alone. There is said to be a butterfly that lives in search of that one flower. That butterfly's flower, that flower's butterfly. They are a unique pair with a bond that lasts through their lifetime. That flower and butterfly couldn't be more different from other flowers; other butterflies. To the human eye, there is nothing more plaintive. To the human heart, there is nothing more loving. It is noble and pure. So what, if tens of thousands of flowers bloom on thousands of mountain peaks? So what, if millions of butterflies visit tens of thousands of planters? Without you, there is no me. Without me, there is no you. You are me and I am you. To realize even the smallest measure of universal compassion is to share a grand and sorrowful love. That flower and butterfly, along with the sun, the moon, and the stars, lead a painstaking existence-they have labored without rest to preserve their species on this planet.

One day, by chance, the poet received a gift from an acquaintance, "several seeds, light as clouds and wind." ("For Absolute Solitude"). In addition to these seeds that are like teardrops and dew, he learned about their history. The poet had always loved mountains and rivers, trees and plants, and all creatures whether they lived in the sky, on land, or in the water. So, for him, the seeds were not a felicitous gift. Although he had a, "tiny planter in [his] corner of this sprawling city," he judged it an unsuitable home for the seeds. No matter how much this butterfly loves this flower, it would be impossible for the butterfly to find its way to this cold and unfamiliar place. And what had the flower done wrong that it would be left to spend its life waiting tearfully, helplessly, for the butterfly that would never come? The more he thought about it, the more he was gripped by an empathy that made it difficult to part with the seeds. In the end, "though spring came and went, [he] did not bury the seeds." In essence, at the heart of Lee Sangguk's poetry is a deep empathy for others, evidenced brilliantly in this poetry collection. Empathy and its variation, love, fill this collection. The flesh and bones of these poems vibrate with life. Painful, yet tender. Painstaking, yet warm.

The cart of poetry that Lee Sangguk has drawn for nearly 50 years has two emotional wheels. One wheel is formed by what was learned by breathing in Mother Nature, and the other wheel is formed by sentiments that form by growing up in an agrarian society. These two emotional wheels carry two loves. One love is formed from the natural sense of community that rises from the belief that all life on this earth is one. The other love is embodied in agrarian communities, in these communal societies where there is no "you" or "I," people simply share and help one another. These two loves form a strong axle. Lee has drawn his cart of poetry along this journey called life armed these two energies; these sentiments and loves. All the while, he gathered stories of the people he met and the world's histories. Accordingly, with each poem Lee mixes and kneads emotion, love, and stories into one body; one poem. The face of his poetry is pure and has a beautiful heart. His poems are vivid proof of his ability to recount life's journey with all its turns. This collection is no different.

The universe's greatest teachings unceasingly stress the importance of love. Joyful love is love, yet sad love is always a focus point. Anyone can experience a joyful love, but a sad love is more difficult to fulfill. It has been said that true love is choosing to be with a poor person and throwing everything away to live in poverty together. This can be seen in the works of Shin Young-bok. Love is to get rained on together, it is not sharing or giving away an umbrella. To share or give away is an altruistic perspective. True love is "to be in the rain together." That is the path to realizing a love without hierarchy. In this way, we can achieve a world that is level; that is peaceful and equal. The people who have walked this path have largely offered up their blood and their lives. We call them holy, saints, righteous. That is how inevitable and how great the accompanying suffering will be. Yet the poet's eye, his heart never strays from the path.

On the road, // even in the rain pooled in cows' hoofprints // clouds drift by, the stars of the night sky shine,// and nameless bugs live on.
—Full text of "Sky Lake"

In Mencius, there is a passage, "All the world's rivers and oceans and lakes are no different to puddles that form on the street after heavy rain." Of course, this is also a metaphor to explain transcendental figures of Confucius, but its meaning is significant. Everything in the world is equal and one. Although it is nothing more than "rain pooled in cows' hoofprints," and has no running source in the way of rivers and oceans, the poem expresses the view that these waters are one in the same. "Sky Lake" shows a viewpoint of discovery. To cast a loving eye on the world is to discover the world's creatures are equal and interconnected. Kneaded into Lee Sangguk's poetry is a common face and inner imagery. He takes stories from the darkness, the damp, the depths, the outcasts, and brings them up into the light and warmth. What's more, he calls them into this world and instills in them the warmth of living as part of a community. It is the reason why his poems have a warm energy in each bend of life it wraps into. It is at the core of his 50-year-long vision.

Love is the source of all sorrow in this world. Where love is damaged, sadness fills its space. There are largely two ways a person's love turns into sadness. One way is destined by the heavens, brought about by ill-fate, as though a calamity or natural disaster has struck. The other way is caused by the human world's greed, it is calculated and violent. Sadness goes hand in hand with pain. At the same time, that pain creates the will to overcome sadness. It is the power of sadness that one does not simply surrender to grief but instead tries to restore love. That is also the power of poetry. It is the melody to the song Lee Sangguk sings as he draws his cart of poetry. This collection of poems which is carried out to the world is no different. It is the fruition of his efforts to return love to its rightful place and make it whole again. The light and fragrant scent of tears can be sensed. "I am from that country and / when rice is threshed I can smell it cooked / and the aroma gives me strength." ("That Country"). The collection is a pure and perfect prescription to heal the world of its "Love fractured, / wounds nobody sees. / Ah, as if washed." ("As if Washed").

PRAISES FOR
LEE SANGGUK

POET

Lee Sangguk's *The House is Still Warm* is a well-structured and fully realized poetry collection. Not a word goes astray, and while his words are simple, they are also dignified and taut. This collection could be categorized as folk poetry rooted in rural and agricultural sentiment, but there are several ways this collection distinguishes itself from others in the genre. Essentially, in his laconic way, he refuses clich?. He does not lean on familiar emotions, nor does he resort to using language that makes an appeal for agreement. This poetry collection raises the level of the genre and points to a new direction by changing the framework and narratives. Other merits of this poetry collection include the way the poetics of so-called modernist poetry are well applied to unexpected subjects. Additionally, Lee is able to engage with goodness and Tao without having to explicitly name them. His language transcends and he ably elevates even the familiar and common.

—Hwang Hyun-san **(literary critic), from the judges' commentary of the 1st Baek Seok Literary Award**

The heart of Lee Sangguk's poetry is kind and holds a gentle sorrow. Rather than siding with the victors of the world, he stands with the losing side, yet treats the world with generosity and forgiveness. It is the kind of sorrow that I feel and empathize with deeply.

—Kim Namjo, **from the judges' commentary of the 24th Chong Chi-Yong Literary Award**

Lee Sangguk's works are rooted in the lyricism of rural life and the lives of common folk, and are conveyed by a plain voice and masculine tone. His poems embody the sincerity that is characteristic of his world of poetry, and his works read with familiarity while evoking a wide-reaching empathy.

—Kim Kwang-kyu (poet), from the judges' commentary of the 2nd Park Jaesam Literary Award

The language of Lee Sangguk is the language of monologue, which bravely and steadfastly battles against the violent power of the dominant language. His language of monologue is not pessimistic, nor is it self-ramblings with no reverberations. His language wholeheartedly believes in the world's natural order. It is the language of nature and, at the same time, it is the language of hope that can escape from the prison of that language.

—Ban Kyung-hwan "The Language of Silence and the Language of Monologue," *Initium Poet Beginning*, Vol. 13

With its clear composition, looking at Lee Sangguk's canvas feels like reading a scholar's poem. At times concise, at times appearing idealistic. Though he seems relaxed and at peace, his judgment is troubled. He is unhappy about the twisting of reality and hates businessmen who look out only for their interests. What he loves is the sunset's hazy hollowness, eating pork skin and drinking soju with friends, and chard soup stewed with blind anchovies.

— Ahn Do-Hyun, from the book blurb for *Someone Who Can't Turn Back Even When It Gets Dark* (Changbi, 2021)

K-POET
Song of the Mushroom

Written by Lee Sangguk
Translated by Deborah Kim
Published by ASIA Publishers
Address 445, Hoedong-gil, Paju-si, Gyeonggi-do, Korea
(Seoul Office: 161-1, Seodal-ro, Dongjak-gu,Seoul, Korea)
Email bookasia@hanmail.net
ISBN 979-11-5662-317-5 (set) | 979-11-5662-719-7 (04810)
First published in Korea by ASIA Publishers 2024

*This book is published with the support of the Literature Translation Institute of Korea (LTI Korea).

Through literature, you
bilingual Edition Modern

ASIA Publishers' carefully selected

Set 1
- Division
- Industrialization
- Women

Set 2
- Liberty
- Love and Love
- Affairs
- South and North

Set 3
- Seoul
- Tradition
- Avant-Garde

Set 4
- Diaspora
- Family
- Humor

Search "bilingual edition

can meet the real Korea!
Korean Literature

22 keywords to understand Korean literature

Set 5

Relationships

Discovering

Everyday Life

Taboo and Desire

Set 6

Fate

Aesthetic Priests

The Naked in the Colony

Set 7

Colonial Intellectuals Turned "Idiots"

Traditional Korea's Lost Faces

Before and After Liberation

Korea After the Korean War

korean literature"on Amazon!

K-픽션 시리즈 | Korean Fiction Series

〈K-픽션〉 시리즈는 한국문학의 젊은 상상력입니다. 최근 발표된 가장 우수하고 흥미로운 작품을 엄선하여 출간하는 〈K-픽션〉은 한국문학의 생생한 현장을 국내외 독자들과 실시간으로 공유하고자 기획되었습니다. 〈바이링궐 에디션 한국 대표 소설〉 시리즈를 통해 검증된 탁월한 번역진이 참여하여 원작의 재미와 품격을 최대한 살린 〈K-픽션〉 시리즈는 매 계절마다 새로운 작품을 선보입니다.

001 버핏과의 저녁 식사-**박민규** Dinner with Buffett-**Park Min-gyu**
002 아르판-**박형서** Arpan-**Park hyoung su**
003 애드벌룬-**손보미** Hot Air Balloon-**Son Bo-mi**
004 나의 클린트 이스트우드-**오한기** My Clint Eastwood-**Oh Han-ki**
005 이베리아의 전갈-**최민우** Dishonored-**Choi Min-woo**
006 양의 미래-**황정은** Kong's Garden-**Hwang Jung-eun**
007 대니-**윤이형** Danny-**Yun I-hyeong**
008 퇴근-**천명관** Homecoming-**Cheon Myeong-kwan**
009 옥화-**금희** Ok-hwa-**Geum Hee**
010 시차-**백수린** Time Difference-**Baik Sou linne**
011 올드 맨 리버-**이장욱** Old Man River-**Lee Jang-wook**
012 권순찬과 착한 사람들-**이기호** Kwon Sun-chan and Nice People-**Lee Ki-ho**
013 알바생 자르기-**장강명** Fired-**Chang Kang-myoung**
014 어디로 가고 싶으신가요-**김애란** Where Would You Like To Go?-**Kim Ae-ran**
015 세상에서 가장 비싼 소설-**김민정** The World's Most Expensive Novel-**Kim Min-jung**
016 체스의 모든 것-**김금희** Everything About Chess-**Kim Keum-hee**
017 할로윈-**정한아** Halloween-**Chung Han-ah**
018 그 여름-**최은영** The Summer-**Choi Eunyoung**
019 어느 피씨주의자의 종생기-**구병모** The Story of P.C.-**Gu Byeong-mo**
020 모르는 영역-**권여선** An Unknown Realm-**Kwon Yeo-sun**
021 4월의 눈-**손원평** April Snow-**Sohn Won-pyung**
022 서우-**강화길** Seo-u-**Kang Hwa-gil**
023 가출-**조남주** Run Away-**Cho Nam-joo**
024 연애의 감정학-**백영옥** How to Break Up Like a Winner-**Baek Young-ok**
025 창모-**우다영** Chang-mo-**Woo Da-young**
026 검은 방-**정지아** The Black Room-**Jeong Ji-a**
027 도쿄의 마야-**장류진** Maya in Tokyo-**Jang Ryu-jin**
028 홀리데이 홈-**편혜영** Holiday Home-**Pyun Hye-young**
029 해피 투게더-**서장원** Happy Together-**Seo Jang-won**
030 골드러시-**서수진** Gold Rush-**Seo Su-jin**
031 당신이 보고 싶어하는 세상-**장강명** The World You Want to See-**Chang Kang-myoung**
032 지난밤 내 꿈에-**정한아** Last Night, In My Dream-**Chung Han-ah**
Special 휴가중인 시체-**김중혁** Corpse on Vacation-**Kim Jung-hyuk**
Special 사파에서-**방현석** Love in Sa Pa-**Bang Hyeon-seok**